CW00985323

SHIRLEY TURNER:
Doctor, Stalker, Murderer
Volume 4

by **Kelly Banaski**

Crimes Canada:
True Crimes That Shocked The Nation Series

SHIRLEY TURNER:
Doctor, Stalker, Murderer
Volume 4

by **Kelly Banaski**

Crimes Canada
True Crimes That Shocked The Nation Series

ISBN-13: **978-1987902068**
ISBN-10: **1987902068**
Published by:

VP Publication an Imprint of
RJ Parker Publishing, Inc.

Published in Canada

Crimes Canada: True Crimes That Shocked the Nation*Series Introduction*

In this multi-volume series edited by crime historian Dr. Peter Vronsky and true crime author and publisher RJ Parker, some of Canada's most notorious shocking crimes will be described and explored.

Crimes Canada: True Crimes that Shocked the Nation will feature a series of Canadian true crime books published by VP Publication (Vronsky & Parker), an imprint of RJ Parker Publishing, Inc., one of the world's leading Indie publishers of true crime.

Peter Vronsky is the bestselling author of Serial Killers: The Method and Madness of Monsters and Female Serial Killers: How and Why Women Become Monsters while RJ Parker is not only a successful Indie publisher but also the author of books like Serial Killers Abridged: An Encyclopedia of 100 Serial Killers, Social Media Monsters: Internet Killers, Parents Who Killed Their Children: Filicide, and Serial Killer Groupies. Both are Canadians and have teamed up to share shocking Canadian true crime cases not only with fellow Canadian readers but with Americans and world readers as well, who will be shocked and horrified by just how evil and sick "nice" Canadians can be when they go bad.

Finally, the editors invite their established Canadian fellow authors and aspiring authors to submit proposals or manuscripts to VP Publication at CrimesCanada@RJParkerPublishing.com.

VP Publication is a new frontier Indie publisher, offering their published authors a generous royalty agreement payable within three months of publishing and aggressive online marketing support. Unlike many so-called "publishers" that are nothing but vanity presses in disguise, VP Publication does not charge authors in advance for submitting their proposal or manuscripts, nor do we charge authors if we choose to publish their works. We pay you, and pay well.

Enjoy these top rated true crime eBooks from VP Publications **FREE** as part of your Kindle Unlimited subscription. You can read it on your Kindle Fire, on a computer via Kindle Cloud Reader or on any smartphone with the free Kindle reading app.

View All True Crime and Crime Fiction Books by RJ Parker Publishing at the following Amazon Links:

Amazon Kindle - USA
Amazon Kindle - Canada
Amazon Kindle - UK
Amazon Kindle - Australia

Background

There are those one-in-a-million special people in the world that never fail to brighten the days of those around them. These perpetually optimistic people have a quality the rest of us do not. They seem hopeful, even in their darkest moments. An aura of quiet complacency while the universe envelops them everywhere they go and it's contagious. We think of them often and remember them fondly. Andrew Bagby was that type of person. He was able to make everyone he met, knew, and loved feel better about themselves and the world around them, and in the end it killed him.

The bizarre murder case of Andrew Bagby entails far more than death, although it has that threefold. It also brought to light a woefully inept Canadian legal system and the frighteningly dark mental descent of a woman scorned. This case is rife with *What If's* and *If*

Only's, a testament, perhaps, to the lingering emotion still felt for Andrew so many years after his death in 2001.

A documentary [1] on the case, *Dear Zachary, A Letter to a Son about His Father,* created by Andrew's lifelong friend Kurt Kuenne, was nominated for best documentary in 2008. It explains his life and death in painstaking detail from his friends and family. Childhood friends, his parents and the friends and colleagues he made as he travelled his life's road all express not only a heartfelt sadness, but also a deep sense of confusion at the events that led up to and tragically took his life. It all seemed to happen so fast and escalate so quickly. Cruelly, hindsight pointed out all the things everyone noticed but never assumed would lead to his death, leaving everyone in his life with a profound sense of regret and guilt to carry along with their grief for the rest of their own lives.

Andrew Bagby met the woman who killed him, his son and herself, in

Newfoundland, Canada in 1999 while studying medicine at Memorial University Newfoundland. Shirley Turner was 13 years his senior at 41 to his 28. She had already been married and divorced twice, had children, and worked as a schoolteacher when she opted to leave her kids with their respective fathers and pursue a career in medicine.

Shirley Turner

Little is known about Shirley Turner's life before she met Andrew. Those who knew her in those days are curiously close-lipped. Perhaps out of their own guilt and sadness for not recognizing her mental instability and attempting to stop her earlier. Perhaps out of a need to put it all behind them and cut ties with

Shirley and the monster she was and the evil deeds she did. She was born in Wichita, Kansas to a Canadian mother [2] and American father and held dual citizenship. Her parents met in Canada. Her mother was native to the area and her father was an American serviceman stationed at a military base in Newfoundland, Canada. They fell in love, and once he was back in the States, he sent for her and they married.

The couple had four children, two girls and two boys. Shirley began life in the United States but moved with her mother to Newfoundland after her parents' divorce in 1968 when she was seven years old.

Life with her mother and siblings was a frugal and nomadic existence, as was the case for most single mothers in the 60's. Upon coming back to Canada, they first settled in Daniels Harbor and began receiving welfare. Soon after, they migrated to Portland Creek and Parsons Pond. Her mother dated many men, settling down only for short spans before the relationship would deteriorate and she would move on. There were no extras or creature comforts in their lives. They lived hand to mouth on her mother's meager wages.

The limited descriptions of Shirley as a child depict her as not quite a loner but never developing any close friendships, not even with her siblings or other family members. She was often sullen and always bossy. She resolved early and loudly that she would not remain in such a minimalistic environment. There was more to life and she meant to have it. She became very determined to leave Parsons Pond and life on welfare far behind her. And leave she did.

In 1980, she began her undergraduate studies at Memorial University St. Johns campus. She studied science and education her first year but got pregnant with her first child, a boy, in 1981 while home on winter recess. She had maintained a long distance love affair with a boy from Parsons Pond while away at college. She married him and, pregnant, returned to school in 1982 to finish her second year of college.

Her first child was born on July 09, 1982. Shirley refused to acknowledge her first mother-in-law. There are no stories of hateful fights between the two. By all accounts, the mother-in-law gave her the space to be a mother but only wanted to share in the life of her grandchild. Try as she might, Shirley would not allow her to be a part of her grandson's life. Shirley would do petty, silly things like leaving all of the grandmother's many gifts out of the "baby book" and not inviting her to outings. She kept her at arm's length unless there was a need she could fill like babysitting. Oddly enough, this grandmother was the person who claimed Shirley's body and arranged for her burial in Parsons Pond.

The young family spent the summer of 1982 in Parsons Pond and then the three of them packed up and moved to St. John's so Shirley could undertake her third year of college and her husband could run the household and raise the baby. He was a stay-at-home father and Shirley supported the family with her student loans and short-term jobs, usually teaching elementary school. The family returned to the Parsons Pond area in the spring of 1983.

Shirley's education was always her most important objective. According to official reports, she would tell family and friends of her deep desire to enter the medical field because of the perceived money she would garner as a doctor. She never spoke of her burning desire to help her fellow man. There were no heartfelt memories of a sick relative or touching past moment that made her career path known forever. Much more simply, Shirley had searched her knowledge base for what she thought would be the most profitable career possible to escape the extreme poverty of her childhood, and a doctor was what she came up with. She had no misgivings about admitting it to whomever wanted to know. She was going to be a doctor and she was going to have money. You'd better believe it.

The couple had a daughter in April of 1985 while Shirley was working as a science teacher in Labrador City. Things were going well for her and her small family at this time. She was enormously popular with the students and had no real trouble with the staff. This could be considered the most successful time of her life. It was short lived, however.

Moving to Labrador City may or may not have been part of some kind of plan on Shirley's behalf. Before her first marriage, she had a relationship with a fisherman from the area. She began an affair with him in the late 80's. Her husband had went to work for the Iron Ore Company of Canada and maintained long hours. She used the opportunity to take the kids to visit family in Parsons Pond, at least for a time. In reality, she would visit only a few hours and then leave the children with a relative so she could take a ferry to a secret rendezvous with her reunited angler lover. It was quite a trip since he was actually in South Labrador, not far from where she and her family lived. But, to carry out her affair, she had to travel to St. Barbe on the Peninsula's northwest coast to drop off her children and have her fake visit to set up an alibi, then off to Southern Labrador to meet her lover. Afterwards, she would travel back to the Peninsula to pick up the children and then back home to her location in Labrador and, her husband. By all implications, she enjoyed the drama, the complication, the chaos – of it all. She thrived on it. The secrecy and the thought of getting one over, not only on her husband but her children and family, was exciting. It proved to her, if no one else, how smart she was.

Shirley and her first husband separated in 1987, and when her teaching duties were over, she took her kids and moved back to the Parsons Pond area. She qualified for some public assistance and set up house alone with her children in Deer Lake until around 1988 when her divorce was final. She also had an abortion around this time. It is unclear who the father was.

She married the fisherman the same year and the two began living together. Sometimes at his place and sometimes at hers. She started teaching school again at Cow Head and later Deer Lake. She resigned from her last teaching position at Deer Lake Integrated School Board in 1993. The couple had one child, a daughter born on March 08, 1990. The marriage had been going south for some time, however, and the couple permanently separated in March of 1991.

After five years of teaching, Shirley decided it was time to enter her fourth year of undergraduate study. Her two children from her first marriage were eleven and eight years old and her daughter from her second marriage was three when she opted to go away for a year. Official interviews with her family show many questioned her decision. It seemed strange for a young mother to be so willing to take so much time from her children for so long a stretch. Her answer was always the money she would make when she finally earned her degree would be worth it all. She graduated with her bachelor's degree in May of 1994.

In early 1994, right before her graduation, her second husband, estranged since 1991, made the move from Parsons Pond to St. John's to help her take care of the children, not only his own daughter that he shared with Shirley, but also her two older children.

A man she had as a boarder in her home at this time reported to his therapist he had witnessed several instances of abuse in the home. He claimed she was most cruel to her oldest daughter and would slap, verbally abuse and beat her. It bothered him to a point that he moved out.

Social Services investigated Shirley for child abuse accusations but the case was dismissed without ever interviewing her, although they left her three messages according to their own report. When the children were interviewed at school, they did not deny the abuse but showed no visible signs of behavioral problems stemming from abuse or signs of beatings. They did interview her husband and he stated she only used beatings with the belt as a threat tactic. He told authorities that it wasn't his job to discipline the children. That was Shirley's job. They stopped investigating and closed the case in January of 2004. This may be the first instance Canada failed Shirley Turner's children.

She divorced her second husband soon after and despite winning custody of their daughter, returned her and her other children to the custody of their fathers and paternal families. She did not live with or participate in the daily lives of any of her children but, with actions truly telling of her personality, she spent thousands of dollars she had agreed was to be put away for her children's own scholarship funds on her own living expenses as she pursued her education. She told family and friends later when she was discovered that she could pay it all back with the big bucks she was going to make as a doctor.

During her second year of medical school in St. John's, she sent for her children and they lived with her throughout the entire academic year. In the middle of her third year, she announced to her family that her schedule with medical school and its responsibilities had become too much for her to deal with, with three kids. The kids were sent back to their paternal families and have remained there ever since.

A traumatic event, which seemed to mark Shirley's life, occurred in 1998. Her mother, who had had a series of romantic relationships throughout Shirley's childhood, had split from her longtime romantic partner. He stayed with Shirley's mother the longest and she had a daughter/father bond with him she had never had with anyone else. Shortly after the split, he became ill. Her mother moved away but Shirley kept in contact with the man until he died. She sent him money and often attempted to help him with his daily struggles. By all accounts, this time in Shirley's life deeply affected her. It may be the only time she showed emotion toward anyone other than her own family.

By 1999, her medical degrees were finished and Shirley began completing residencies in family medicine and serving as resident physician at teaching hospitals. As years progress, even the most immature and vain person begins to realize that there is more to life than one's own wants and needs. Most people realize at some point in life that their point of view is not the only one available, accurate or necessary. Shirley, however, seemed to grow more narcissistic with each passing year. Time and again, people have stepped forward to tell their unpleasant story of how she was rude, abrasive or downright abusive to them. If she wasn't pissing someone off, she was doing the polar opposite. She could be amazingly charming. Tales abound of Shirley's ability to manipulate and coerce others into giving her what she wanted only for them to realize too late that she was only in it for herself. It was usually when this didn't work that she shifted to more obnoxious behavior.

Her professional behavior was called into question a number of times at various hospitals throughout her residencies. A supervising physician at a hospital in St. John's reported that Turner repeatedly became hostile when disciplined. She would scream, yell, cry, claim unfair treatment and throw accusations at her supervisory physicians when corrected. One supervisor reported that Shirley *had lied right to my face and still forcibly argued her case, accusing me of improper supervision*. He further stated she rebuffed his discipline by stating that no other supervisor had ever had a problem with her work and all evaluations so far had been above average. When the supervisor checked, however, neither statement was true.

Her coworkers and supervisors were leery of her behavior and refused to have conversations with her alone, afraid of how she would later twist it in her own favor somehow. One went so far as to state that he had never before or since been forced to adopt that form of staff management. They describe her as manipulative and psychotic. One patient at the hospital refused to come back after a conflict with Turner, and in another incident she was accused of falsifying attendance documents after missing nine days of a three-month rotation at the hospital. When asked about her absences, she replied she had spent hours tending to a sick child, even though everyone knew her children lived hours away. When pressed, she claimed she had been on the phone with her sick child as well as a local pharmacist because the child's attending physician prescribed the wrong medication. She was never at a shortage of excuses or lies. The fact that people could see right through her lies or knew they were outright lies never seemed to affect her. She would seem indignant that they were not believed without question, ignoring the fact that she lied altogether.

Coworkers, supervisors and patients describe Shirley Turner as abrasive and pushy but at times charming, but in a forced, artificial kind of way. To them, she seemed superficial and incapable of any real connection, and appeared detached and distant. Her supervisors were taken aback at her lack of personal commitment in such a personal career. Her time at the St. John's hospital led the administration to instill "constructive changes" to its residency review process.

The fact that Shirley Turner was a doctor and interacted daily with doctors goes a long way in explaining how difficult sociopathy is to determine. Sociopathic behavior is characterized by the glibness and superficial charm Dr. Turner was well known for. Sociopaths lack remorse and act impulsively. They are highly manipulative and extremely conning. They cannot see past their own cunning noses, so to speak, and they feel everything they do to get their own agenda passed is permissible because they do not recognize the rights of other people.

Shirley Turner was no exception. Her goal to become a doctor and make the big bucks was, to her, the most important thing in the world. She could not, and would not, see anything else as equally important. This included her children, husbands, marriages and relationships. The goals of the people in her life were inconsequential. Nothing mattered but Shirley and what she wanted.

The Female Sociopath

Female sociopaths [3] can be more dangerous than their male counterparts because the world has a hard time accepting them as such. They bewilder the world around them. Dr. Liane Leedom, psychologist and author of the book *Just Like His Father?* [4], explains that women sociopaths are more reviled and fearsome than their male counterparts because women are preprogrammed genetically to be the antithesis of sociopathy. They are geared toward empathy and caretaking. People in general do not expect a woman to be any other way.

According to Dr. Leedom, an indicator of the female sociopath is the lack of care and emotion toward her own children, something clearly present in Shirley's behavior as early as her first child and most obviously in her last. Her goals for her life were always far more important to her than her own children. Female sociopaths tend to be high achievers, perhaps because of their heightened sense of self-importance and their belief that their own journey is more important than that of any other person. Female sociopaths use everyone in their lives to get to where they want to be. They begin by assessing every person they come in contact with, every person in their life, for what that person can do for them. Firstly, by determining their potential victim's weak points. They con the person into feeling comfortable with them by making them believe they truly like whom their victim is and that they themselves are just like them. Eventually the potential victim begins to believe it and they entrust the female sociopath with their secrets, in turn giving them the beginning of their arsenal against them. They carefully and strategically evaluate the weaknesses and strengths, personal traits, values and insecurities of every person they know to find the best way to make them believe they are trustworthy and similar in character to themselves. Once the victim becomes entrapped, the manipulation begins.

A female sociopath may seem like a completely different person with each of her victims[5]. She will wear a "mask" or fake persona tailored to each potential victim's needs in a friend. Her lies are very specifically designed for each person. There is no value in telling the truth for these women unless it can help them achieve a goal. A lie is more often useful for them. Friendships are worn like gloves: to be discarded when the usefulness of the person and their friendship has run its course. Since sociopaths know no real friendships, once this usefulness is exhausted, they will abandon everyone in their lives.

The female sociopath will have an emotional need to justify their actions and behavior. They will seek out the gratitude, love and respect of their victims and ask for it repeatedly. Their need to be important and justified is staggering. They do not perceive any problems with their own actions and are contemptuous of those who seek to understand their behavior much as Dr. Turner did to her residency supervisors. It is when they cannot control their victim's every move that they show their true colors and begin to be violent and cruel. Paranoia reaches extreme levels and they often become more grandiose. In the 1800s, medical science termed this type of personality malady a *moral insanity* [6]. In the 1900s, it was known as a *psychopathic personality* [7] and in recent years it has been termed an antisocial personality disorder. They all mean the same thing, which is a general disregard and non-recognition of legal and moral standards. This behavior is evident in the way Dr. Turner manipulated the judge she wrote to during her incarceration, and the power of female sociopaths is never more evident than in the way the judge catered to her. It shows how good she really was at her deceit.

The Stalking Begins

In mid-2000, Shirley Turner [8] fulfilled all requirements and earned her license to practice medicine. From 1996 until 1999, Dr. Shirley Turner was involved with a resident at St. John's, a man nine years her junior.

It began as a few dates, as most do, and while he thought of it as just a few casual dates, Shirley expected much more. She built the relationship into a monumental love affair in her mind. It lasted only months, but she spent years stalking and harassing him throughout Canada and the United States. They had dated only a short time before her strange behavior and threatening demeanor ran him off. Like many other people in her life, he detected early on that she was unstable, but instead of confronting her or attempting any type of interventions, he tried to walk away. No matter where he went or what he did, she would appear and make a scene, shouting obscenities and accusations. She besieged him with hundreds of phone calls, text messages and voicemails at all hours of the day and night. She stalked him both obviously and incognito. When he moved, she found and followed him and started all over again. She once struck him in the eye with a high-heeled shoe after he moved from Newfoundland to Nova Scotia to escape her. Perhaps it shows just how desperate he was to avoid her when he moved to Pennsylvania, United States in 1998. This was no deterrent to her, since she held dual citizenship, and again, she followed him. Again, she flooded him with phone calls and voicemails, threatening to stab, kill and bury him six feet under. Eventually, she began to make unannounced visits to his home from which she had to be escorted away by the Pennsylvania State Police. Finally, in an elaborate display on an April morning in 1999, Dr. Shirley Turner was found semi-conscious in a black dress carrying a bouquet of red roses on the curb outside his home.

She had been ordered to see and had subsequently been an outpatient of a psychiatrist sometime earlier in the relationship. In her pocket the morning she was found outside his home were two suicide notes; one was for the psychiatrist, the other for the man. In it, she proclaimed that she was not evil, only sick, which leads one to believe that she knew she was wrong and getting worse. The following day, the man found one last voicemail from Dr. Turner. The voice was clearly hers but she was attempting to disguise it and give a message that Dr. Turner had died. This is the woman who met young, compassionate Dr. Andrew Bagby.

Dr. Andrew Bagby

Andrew Bagby [9] grew up in Sunnyvale, California, a loveable, chubby neighborhood kid who was easy to befriend. He was known for his genuine interest in his friends and family and for the way he tried to help each person he knew in some way. An Eagle Scout for many years and an amateur actor and photographer, his avid interests made him easy to talk to on a number of subjects. He'd had a long time, on-again off-again romance with Heather Arnold, who also became a doctor, before finally calling it completely off and moving on in 1999.

His childhood friends adored him and vice versa. The documentary made by his friend Kurt showed clip after clip of the two starring in Kurt's vignettes. The two teens, their myriad friends and even Andrew's parents acted out the scripts written by Kurt and Andrew, fight scenes, and sophomoric comedy scenes, that now seem strangely prophetic.

Andrew was an only child who seemed to actually like his parents. There was never an issue of drugs or dangerous behavior in his teen years. He remained close to his parents through adulthood. Kate Bagby, Andrew's mother, was a midwife and nurse, and he had dreamed all his life of following her into the medical field. He had already tried and failed to attend medical school previously, with a series of applications and rejections, when he was finally accepted at Memorial University Newfoundland. David Bagby, a computer engineer, had always been supportive of Andrew's goals and dreams, regardless of what they were. Throughout Andrew's life, Kate and David played an active part, participating not only in the amateur movies Andrew and his friend Kurt Kuenne would produce, but also in his scouting, education and social life even after he grew up and went away to college. They kept in close contact with him until the day he died.

When he travelled to Canada for medical school, it was the first time he had been so far from his family and friends. It was a trying time for Andrew, who always held himself as a bit of an outcast, despite his many loving friends. In the documentary, they describe him as self-effacing, often calling himself a short and portly guy. While he was known for his kindness and generosity, his few faults seem to have made him more endearing as evidenced in their tales of his bad gas and terrible nail-biting habits. He was human and each of his fallacies made him seem even more so. He acknowledged them and smiled in the face of each.

Andrew and Shirley met at Memorial University Newfoundland and became friendly. They were often seen together, out and about. In the documentary of the case, *Dear Zachary: A letter to a Son about His Father*, they kiss and seem intimate on camera and, of course, she eventually becomes pregnant with his baby, and yet his friends describe them as seemingly casual. On camera, his friends say she seemed incongruous to the type of women he was attracted to. Andrew loved women, and as most heterosexual men his age, he talked about them. He commented on the women he found beautiful and lamented his chances on those he felt were out of his league. But yet he never spoke of Shirley. She just seemed to begin appearing at his side one day. The age difference glaringly obvious, his friends were confused but too polite to say anything. Andrew's split from Heather Arnold had been hard for him, and they all wanted nothing more than for him to find someone he enjoyed being with and could share his life with. Around his friends, she was aloof and slightly disgruntled, obviously bitter at sharing his time with others. Despite announcing they were a couple, he was not affectionate toward her. His friends chalked the relationship up to his long span in medical school spent so far from home. Shirley's incessant attempts to spend time with him seemed like something he appreciated in a desperate time and they tolerated her for that reason.

The people who knew them best claim they seemed an unnatural match, that something felt wrong about them. Shirley had a crude sense of humor, was ill-mannered, dirty-minded and often unkempt, this in sharp contrast to the personable, kind and tidy Andrew.

She had a fierce and obvious jealous streak and went so far as to call Andrew's old girlfriend Heather Arnold and explain to her how much more Andrew loved her than he had

Heather and spin romantic tales of their glorious, unbounded love. The very fact that Heather once held a place in Andrew's heart drove Shirley to distraction. She catered to an overpowering compulsion to prove to Heather that she meant nothing to Andrew. These phone calls never ended without a veiled threat and an ominous tone.

When one of his friends got married and Andrew hadn't invited her as a guest, she put in call upon call to his cell phone and home phone complaining loudly and violently until he turned off his phone only to come home to over 30 volatile messages. Friends witness to this tirade commented on his amazing tolerance and ability to just shake his head dismissively, but they could tell he was embarrassed and aggravated. Andrew's countenance was not one of confrontation.

Never in his life had he treated anyone cruelly and he'd never had to. Shirley was the first instance in his life when he'd suddenly been confronted with the issue. Here was a woman constantly and blatantly disregarding his good will and even using it against him. She knew he was a kindhearted person and she used it to her benefit, knowing he had a hard time being mean to someone, even those who deserved it. There is a line in the documentary from one of his friends – Andrew didn't know how to be a son of a bitch, because he wasn't a son of a bitch.

He acquiesced and invited her to a friend's wedding in October of 2001, where he served as best man. The wedding video shows them dancing, her crazily hanging on him and twirling about with lascivious moves and him oddly stiff and uncomfortable. A female friend asked if he'd like a drink and Shirley embarrassingly accused her of "hitting on the best man". She was feeling Andrew's attempt at pulling away and reacted with a fierce possessiveness.

Friends and family share feelings of unease over the couple in the documentary. It is perhaps, for all these reasons, the relationship began to wane and falter within two years.

In 2000, Shirley moved to Iowa to pursue a career in medicine at Trimark Physicians Corporation in Sac City. Her two oldest children were becoming adults themselves. Her oldest son, needing money for college, requested the "baby bonuses" she had been receiving and had told her family she'd socked away for her children's education. She had to admit that she'd spent them, making her family furious. He worked his way through school with part-time restaurant jobs and, in student loans. Shirley's oldest daughter was around 15 years old at this time and was involved with a boy who had moved to Ontario. The daughter longed to be with him and continue the romantic relationship and asked her mother for help. Shirley agreed and in an unusual move for a mother, allowed her 15-year-old daughter to move to Ontario to persue a romantic relationship, giving her $700 for homeschooling instruction. Had Child

Protective Services been paying attention, this could have allowed them a peek into Dr. Turner's life and possibly stopped her madness. This is another instance the Canadian childcare system failed Dr. Turner's children.

Andrew told friends they were no longer romantically involved at this point but had remained close friends. While no one can be sure at this point, he must have been sleeping with her in some way he hoped was casual. He had no real way of knowing that Shirley was incapable of just being friends with a former lover. This wasn't something Shirley could do.

Shirley maintained to all who inquired and many who didn't that they were attempting a long-distance relationship. She had, in fact, visited his home a number of times during this strange period, but Andrew had visited her home only once.

The year 2000 was also the year Andrew Bagby graduated from Memorial University Newfoundland. His dream finally realized, he began searching out a compatible residency. He quickly garnered one in New York at State University of New York at Syracuse. He hated the surgical residency. Shirley was a constant presence, even from a distance and, although he knew he didn't want to be with her, his kind nature and his miserable state at the residency made it hard to be completely cold to her.

Shirley began to act as though she had forgotten she and Andrew had split. In fact, she behaved as if it had never happened. Her jealousy and possessive behavior began slowly to reignite. Her sociopathic tendencies were amping up again. Things didn't work out to Andrew's satisfaction with Shirley or the residency so he moved to Pennsylvania to begin a residency, at a small family practice. In hindsight, those who knew them say they should have noticed how much of an effect Shirley had on Andrew during this time. No one knew her history and the incident with the young intern in St. John's. No one knew her tendency to stalk and follow ex-lovers across entire countries. Certainly, no one could have predicted what she would do next.

Around this time is when things start to get weird. Andrew had moved to Latrobe, Pennsylvania to begin his residency. He enjoyed the position and became close to his supervisory physician, Dr. T. Clark Simpson. He confided in him about his problems with Shirley and her increasingly weird behavior. Dr. Simpson became a close friend and confidant, privy to the unusual threats and stalking behavior of Shirley Turner. He worried for Andrew. He advised Andrew to call the police if the behavior continued, but Andrew balked. "What could happen?" he asked his friend.

As the relationship between Andrew and Shirley became more and more volatile and uncomfortable, Andrew withdrew and Shirley pressed characteristically forward. As with her stalking of the young resident at St. John's, she began to call insistently. She left messages and threats over and over again. She made unannounced visits, secretly watched his comings and goings, and when Andrew started dating someone new, she began to leave her threatening messages as well.

Shirley left Sac City and moved to Council Bluffs, Iowa for a position at Alegent Health Systems. She also bought a gun and began lessons on how to use it. All the while calling, threatening and, secretly and not so secretly, visiting Andrew Bagby. On November 3rd of 2001, Andrew Bagby had had enough. Shirley had flown down to see him on the pretense of friendship although he had told her he didn't want her to. The visit was unpleasant, to say the least. She didn't seem to understand they were not a couple and demanded explanations for why he was dating and why he wasn't answering her calls and messages. At the advice of Dr. Simpson, he drove Dr. Shirley Turner to the airport and, for the first time and out of character, broke off any and all communication in no uncertain terms. He was finished. Emotionally and physically drained, he simply could not do it any longer. He told her he never wanted to see her again.

The Murder of Andrew

Early the next day, November 4, Shirley Turner [10] placed several calls to Andrew's residence. When he did not answer, she left her home and drove the more than 1,300 miles to Andrew's residence where she confronted him in the early morning hours of November 5th on his way to work. In her Toyota RAV4 was the gun and ammunition she had bought and been practicing with in the preceding weeks. When he insisted he had to go to work, she demanded he meet her after to talk. He promised to meet her at the Keystone State Park later in an attempt to get her to leave so he could go on to work. She stayed in his residence, across the street from his modest medical office, under the supervision of Dr. T. Clark Simpson as he walked across the street to work. His agitated state alerted Dr. Simpson who asked about Bagby's condition. "You'll never guess who showed up on my doorstep this morning." He reportedly said. When

Simpson asked who, he replied "That psychotic bitch." Andrew explained that he'd driven her to the airport with instructions never to return and stay out of his life on the 3rd only to have her call ceaselessly and then show up. Simpson again suggested he call the police and refuse to meet her anywhere. The documentary shows him saying he told Andrew if a woman showed up at his front door after cutting it off in such a manner, he would be going out the back door. If only Andrew had taken this last bit of advice. Instead, he promised to contact Simpson at his home later in the evening after his meeting with Shirley Turner. According to Dr. Simpson, Andrew called before the meeting and said "Its 4:30 now. Im meeting her at six. Seven thirty I'll be at your house." He never fulfilled that promise.

The next morning, November 6, 2001, Andrew did not show up to work. By the end of morning report, around 8:30 a.m., Andrew still hadn't shown up. Dr. Simpson began calling Andrew's phones. Shortly after nine a.m., news reports began airing of a body found in scrubs at the state park, and his coworkers braced themselves for the worst. It wasn't long before the police arrived and gathered the staff together for the terrible news. Dr. Simpson immediately began to tell them about Shirley and the events of the night before.

On November 6, 2001, Dr. Andrew Bagby was found dead in a parking lot for day use at Keystone State Park in Derry Township, Pennsylvania. He had been shot to death. There were five gunshot wounds as well as blunt force trauma to the back of the head. He had been shot in both the face and chest as well as the back of the head, back and buttocks. He was left face down in the parking lot in his scrubs, next to his Toyota Corolla. He died there.

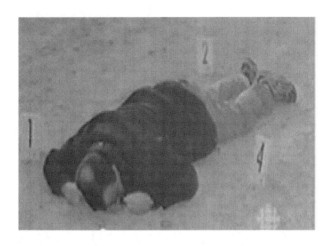

When police contacted Shirley Turner in Iowa, she claimed to have been at home all along. She made those claims knowing she had made cell phone calls before, during and after her drive to Andrew's home. She had also checked into several online accounts from his home computer, including eBay. She used his home phone to call in sick to work. Lies, right off the bat, are always a telling sign from the defense, but even if she'd told them she'd seen Andrew, the evidence already pointed to her as the shooter. When confronted with her lies, she confessed to meeting Andrew at the state park.

She also said she gave Andrew the gun she'd purchased, which matched the spent and unspent shell casings at Andrew's death scene, and he put it in his trunk. In another story, she couldn't find it, and in yet another she had told to her shooting instructor, it had been stolen.

The more people police interviewed, the worse it looked for Dr. Shirley Turner. Not only had she lied to the police initially about her whereabouts, but she'd also lied about the gun. She told police Andrew had it in his trunk but she told her gun instructor it had been stolen, as she testified to police. Mountains of evidence were building against her. In the same police interview with Shirley's gun instructor, he explained that her specific gun ejected live rounds on occasion. This matched the crime scene, as live rounds matching the type Shirley used were found along with spent ones on the ground around Andrew's body.

A witness then came forward who was walking through the park and saw Andrew's car parked next to Shirley's car ten minutes before his last cell phone call to Dr. Simpson. The same witness saw Andrew's car in the same spot the next morning, all alone. Police found a box of condoms in Shirley's apartment that matched a box of condoms purchased by Andrew the night he sent her back to Iowa on a plane. There were also MapQuest directions to Andrew's town found in Shirley's apartment.

Andrew's friends put together a memorial service for him and, despite knowing she was a suspect, and knowing everyone else did too, Shirley attended. She cried loudly and flagrantly. When Heather Arnold showed up to speak about her friend and ex-fiancé, Shirley did not miss the opportunity to sidle in next to her and let her know how little she meant to Andrew, how much more he loved her and how their love will not be stopped by mere death. She followed it up with bitter scathing emails along the same vein.

Escape to Canada

While evidence was steadily mounting against her, Dr. Shirley Turner dropped everything, left her car, apartment and every worldly possession, and went back to Canada.

By the time Pennsylvania had an open warrant on her, she was in St. John's, Newfoundland, Canada. Andrew's parents, Kate and David Bagby, invited her to their son's memorial in an attempt to bring her back to face justice, but she did not show up. Instead, she trumped their memorial service with a real life memorial, announcing she was four months pregnant with Andrew's baby.

The U.S. was in the middle of the extradition process with Canada to bring her back, but she was not held in custody. She gave birth to a boy she named Zachary, son of Andrew Bagby, and went home to fight her extradition.

David and Kate Bagby had moved to Canada while awaiting the birth of the baby and Shirley's extradition. Just as Shirley had done, they quit their jobs, dropped everything and moved to another country. Shirley would not allow them into the visiting room while she was in labor and delivery. She refused to let them see little Zachary when he was born. She attempted to freeze them out altogether but was not prepared for their tenacity. They fought for visiting rights and gained the right to see him one hour a week. Shirley was terrified of how they would talk to her son about her, so she insisted on being present for every visit. They wanted custody of Zachary and hoped to gain it when their son's killer finally went to jail. They increasingly wondered just when that would be.

Court dates were postponed, motions denied, hearings unheard and Shirley remained a free woman. They waited more. They waited as her lawyer thwarted attempt after attempt to jail her. Eventually, when a provincial court decided there was indeed enough evidence to prove Shirley Turner killed Andrew Bagby, she was arrested.

The Bagbys were finally awarded custody of baby Zachary, with Shirley's blessing, although they had to drive him to visit her once a week. She seemed to know that while she hated the fact that they were his guardians, it could serve some purpose for her. For a short time, Zachary and his grandparents made a happy family. Despite the absence of his father, the Bagbys kept him alive for his son. They talked of him every day and many of his childhood friends travelled to meet him, including filmmaker Kurt Kunne. Shirley would call the Bagbys from jail, which they recorded. Her voice a high-pitched whine, her emotions sounding forced and flat, she would complain that she felt the Bagbys would turn Zachary away from her one minute and dish out back-handed compliments the next.

She would thank them for their help and then complain Zachary's lack of attention at their jail visits were because they were secretly turning him against her. Her comments, while sickeningly sweet, were meant to cut. In a recorded conversation from jail, she asked the Bagbys if they would consider hanging a photo of her and Andrew in Zachary's room, in a frame stamped with Mommy and Daddy upon it. David Bagby is heard saying they, especially Kate, were not quite there yet. Shirley's passive-aggressive response was to request they get help and mention she could not agree to extended custody upon her release if they didn't learn to deal with it. She would allude to how she planned to get custody back and attempt to be manipulative, but David Bagby would shut her down every time. Over and over he told her they would not discuss Andrew, the murder or any of the circumstances with her.

He pointedly and repeatedly reminded her they would have no relationship and no conversations other than those pertaining to the health and well-being of their grandson.

Shirley's narcissistic and sociopathic personality would not allow her to accept this and she kept trying. It's hard to gauge what her intentions were, what she really hoped to achieve by this torment. Did she really want their approval and love or was it just a sick ploy to dangle the only grandchild of their only son in their face?

The one prominent thought the general public has upon getting intimate with this case is the unbelievable strength the Bagbys maintained. From the moment they moved to Canada, they had to interact and be cordial to the woman who shot their son down in the street and was walking around free for the most part. They had to make idle chitchat about diapers and baby food and the weather, all the while looking into the face of their son's murderer. First, watching her appear in court pregnant, knowing it was their only grandchild inside the murderous, insane woman. The evidence was overwhelming, the United States had sent explicit warning, and the case undeniably strong, and yet Dr. Shirley Turner remained unfazed. No one seemed to realize or care that she was a murderer, a cold-blooded murderer.

While in jail, she wrote to a judge. Against legal precedent, this judge wrote her back and gave her legal advice on how to proceed with her case. The United States presented evidence of her crimes and their investigation and findings thus far. It was overwhelming. Her lies were exposed, her gun casings matched and witnesses placed her car next to his at the time of the murder. What happened next is one of the strangest decisions in legal history.

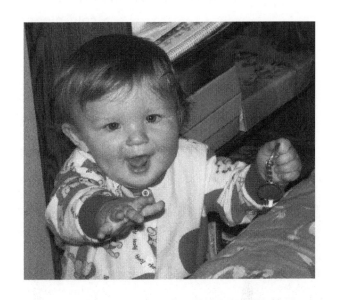

Murderer Granted Bail

Newfoundland judge Gale Welsh decided Dr. Shirley Turner, the woman who shot and killed Andrew Bagby, was no threat to society and set her free on $75,000 bail, $65,000 of which her psychologist, Dr. John Doucet, paid in a legally questionable move for which he was later brought up on charges. In 2006, he was found guilty of professional misconduct and fined $10,000 as well as ordered to undergo psychiatric counselling himself. Bailing her out while she was under his care was deemed a violation of doctor/patient ethics. The Bagbys were elated, as they saw this move as largely responsible for Zachary's death.

Judge Welsh received statements from the state of Pennsylvania that Shirley had psychotic tendencies, that she was possibly suicidal, there were eight restraining orders against her, the various stalking charges, and the crime scene evidence. The judge was not swayed and stated her belief that Shirley's anger and violence was directed toward one person and that person was dead, so she was not a threat to anyone anymore, at least not to the public in general. She further went on to say there was no evidence of a psychological issue despite what the U.S. had presented. Finally, she cited Dr. Turner's divine right to be presumed innocent and placed it above the safety of young Zachary.

Shirley regained partial custody once she reentered the free world. The relationship between her and the Bagbys was strained. Zachary visibly preferred his grandmother to his mother and it upset Shirley. Still shots and video in the documentary show a smiling, happy baby Zach until his mother comes near. His smile fades and he squirms and fidgets to be free. Only to run straight to the arms of his grandmother. Shirley's voice is a comical take on what an over-attentive, loving mom would sound like, if one had been present. Shirley would try to interfere with the Bagbys' scheduled times with one excuse after another, claiming scheduling issues or just outright jealousy. She made the same old accusations and grew increasingly agitated when they would not succumb to her demands and manipulations.

Somehow, she managed to garner a new boyfriend during this melee, and when the new man in her life saw some news reports of her legal issues, he promptly dumped her. She slid down the slippery slope of sociopathic psychosis once more. Claiming a fraudulent pregnancy, she racked up another 200 cell phone calls to him all the while fighting extradition almost on a daily basis.

Murder / Suicide

On August 18, 2003, [11] Shirley went uninvited to the new boyfriend's home, leaving tampons and photos to mark her presence. She called a friend and made it known where she was. Authorities believe she may have been contemplating framing the boyfriend for what she did next.

At that point, she went home and poured up to 30 tablets of the prescription medicine Ativan [12] into Zachary's formula bottle, taking several doses herself. Dr. Shirley Turner then drove to Kelligrews, a small municipality on the Conception Bay coast where she strapped 13-month old Zachary to her chest and jumped into the Atlantic Ocean. Both she and Zachary drowned and were washed ashore separately where two tourists found them the next day.

The Bagbys first assumed Shirley had absconded with Zachary and waited on pins and needles for hours as authorities searched for the pair. They faced the brutal truth late the next day when the bodies surfaced. Once again, David and Kate experienced the death of a child they had loved and raised by the same murderous hand. Their pain immobilized them for weeks, months. They sought privacy from the press. Although they contemplated dual suicide, in the end they chose to fight.

Illustration 1: Picture taken by RJ Parker on May 25, 2015 from Topsail Bluff which overlooks Manuel Beach, Conception Bay, Newfoundand.

Battling The Legal System

The Bagby's took on the Canadian legal system [13] in a fight to change the country's bail laws, which they blame for Zachary's death, and Newfoundand's Ministry of Justice agreed with them. A series of questions that were asked to the Office of Child and Youth Advocacy shows that the many events that would seem to serve as red flags raised no attention. Shirley had even contacted the office before she was incarcerated and inquired as to what she could do for her child. The sadness and despondency stayed with them. They did not decorate for holidays or celebrate as others did. They put up small shrines to Andrew and Zachary in their home and resigned themselves to the pain that never goes away, determined to make the deaths of their loved ones mean something.

The Bagbys refused to let things lie, however, and insisted on making changes that would prevent similar instances in the future. Although many things seemed to need attention, the Bagbys had one law in mind. That one fateful day still weighed heavy on their hearts, the day they truly felt as though the legal system had failed them, was the target of their attempts. If it wasn't for the judge's questionable decision to uphold Shirley's presumption of innocence, despite the heavy evidence against her, baby Zachary may not have met his untimely end. The Bagbys therefore, had bail reform on the mind. When the emotionally wrecked grandparents heard that Shirley had been released on bail, they decided to hold a press conference in an attempt to gain public attention and support. Although they had been warned that a press ban was still in place, they decided to go ahead with the conference in which they spoke of the terrible story of Andrew and Zachary and how they felt the government was to blame.

The news of Shirley's release combined with the questionable payment made by her psychologist was too much for the Bagbys to handle. They thought for sure that the ordeal would be settled before she was released on bail and afterwards felt utterly helpless. The press conference helped very little other than to express their feelings. With the government seeming to work against them, the Bagbys didn't know what else to do to aid the process. In the documentary, they expressed how frantic thoughts would cross their minds about kidnapping poor Zachary and going on the run. The overworked couple would sit and, with nothing left to do, they'd contemplate potential escape routes with the child. Where they would go and how they would get there was all they thought about. Finally, their wildest dreams of running away were busted by the realization that to run would entail hiring a private boat for transportation. The deed that put them in this situation crossed David's mind, murder. David, in his distraught state of mind, even considered leaving in the dead of night to go and, as he put it, take care of things himself. He planned to leave while Kathleen was sleeping and tell her nothing of his plans to avoid her persecution in the incidence of his arrest.

After the murders, Kathleen and David, despite now feeling as though their efforts had been in vain, continued their quest for justice. Among their attempts to change bail and child protection laws, they also held group support meetings for victims of similar crimes. Finally, in 2006, Peter H. Markesteyn launched a full-scale investigation of the case and how the Office of Child and Youth Advocacy group [14] had failed to protect young Zachary. The first attempts at contacting Lloyd Wicks, the main authority over OCYA were not rewarded. In the end, Mr. Wicks denied an interview, but agreed to answer some questions through a letter. With this information, many discoveries were made and it was realized that the child protective services needed drastic change. The OCYA had failed to question the fact that a woman charged with murder was responsible for a young child. Mr. Wicks admitted to not having knowledge of Shirley's case through her interaction with the organization but instead only possessed what was gathered through media sources, meaning that although Shirley had herself spoken with the office, no one was alerted. Further evidence of the office's shortcomings was gained when Mr. Wicks was asked about any services rendered to Shirley and young Zachary. Time and time again, the office's lack of action became clear. The OCYA, in some form, had been in contact with Shirley and had failed to provide them with any services whatsoever. Once the department had become aware of Shirley's situation, information about her case could have been obtained.

This information, for obvious reasons, deeply troubled the Bagbys. They had repeatedly attempted to alert the government of Shirley's murder accusation in the U.S., her previous history of violence and sociopathic tendencies, and the fact that she was in possession of the child. The Bagbys even expressed that their own background was not checked at previous times when taking custody of Zachary. They said in the documentary that it seemed as though anyone could have claimed to be guardian of a child and win custody in that time period. The experience they had with the government as well as the OCYA's lack of action on Shirley's case motivated them ever more to accomplish change. They felt that not only did the government fail to uphold their legal duty and purpose to protect Zachary, but also failed to uphold a moral standard to inquire about the safety of the child when the extreme nature of the case was brought to their attention. The lack of action was not only on the provincial level, but also at a federal level as they would later come to realize.

When the 15-month case review was completed, Mr. Markesteyn concluded that the office was indeed negligent of their duties. No clear explanation exists for what happened or why the terrible situation was not caught, just as the many other instances of Shirley's neglect and abuse of her children slipped through the cracks in the provincial child care laws. In the report, Markesteyn laid out 56 suggestions of reforms to be made to the child protection laws of Canada.

After ten years of lobbying, it paid off. The documentary, *Dear Zachary: A letter to a Son about His Father,* was a big part of the success. Originally meant for Zachary as a memoir of his father, the filmmaker and Andrew Bagby's childhood best friend, Kurt Kuenne, began recording favorite memories of Andrew Bagby by his friends and family. Kuenne was one of several neighborhood boys who grew up and went to college with Andrew in Sunnyvale, California. During the course of filming, however, Shirley Turner did her terrible deed. The documentary then turned into a sort of crime drama, with elements of a Hollywood thriller. Throughout the film are pauses in the action in which narration meant to be heard by Zachary explains what is happening with a soft tone meant to soften the blow landed by the terrible nature of the news. The narration is always phrased as though he were speaking to Andrew's son, adding to the film's eye-watering quality. The documentary is a truly touching story. Near the end of the film at the point when Zachary's body was found, the voice of Andrew's childhood friend reappears. He speaks of the heartbreaking discovery. He contemplated giving up on the film since the purpose was to deliver the film to Zachary as a testament to the many people who helped to bring his father's murderer, his own mother, to justice. It masterfully displayed the glaring misconduct by the Canadian legal system along with the frightening mental descent of Shirley Turner. David Bagby wrote every Member of Parliament and senator and offered a private screening of the film. He reached out to public relations consultant and lobbyist, Gord McIntosh, to help promulgate the idea, and the pair were relentless.

Coroner Peter Markesteyn [15] released a three-volume report in 2006 in which he patently blamed deeply rooted flaws in the province's social services for what he called Zachary's preventable death. He stated that the presumption of innocence mistakenly played a bigger role in the case than the safety of Zachary. His report and the documentary went a long way in the passing of the bill.

Immediately after, Newfoundland and Labrador Child and Youth Advocate, Darlene Neville, began a no-holds-barred investigation into the fundamental policies of the child welfare system and was shocked at the results. She made statements to the press regarding her apprehension for the welfare of other children currently in the system in similar circumstances. She marveled at how out of touch the entire organization was with reality and stated that two things were glaringly obvious after studying the investigation findings; that Zachary should not have been in the care of his mother and his death was preventable. The outcome being that if the same amount of resources, time and effort from the child welfare system had been put into Zachary's rights and protection as had been given Shirley, he would still be alive.

In 2007, David Bagby wrote a book called *Dance with the Devil: A Memoir of Murder and Loss* in which he detailed the crimes of Dr. Shirley Turner and the terrible losses it caused. While the touching documentary showed the story from a friend's point of view, David's book showed the intense emotional and physical beatings the story doled out on family. It begins with the stories of Andrew and Zachary and their tragic end, but the true heart of the book is the journey to make the bail law a reality. It goes into great, technical detail of the bill's origin, its fight and progression to become law. Along with the documentary, this book was used to lobby the bill to Senate and Parliament.

In 2009, a special screening of *Dear Zachary: A letter to a Son about His Father* was held in the capital screening room during which Liberal Sen. Tommy Banks and Liberal MP Scott

Andrews were visibly touched. In the fall of 2009, a private bill, introduced by Newfoundland MP Scott Andrews, proposed an additional clause in the criminal code allowing bail to be denied if deemed necessary to protect a minor. While the bill was a certain success, the Bagbys pressed on. They had envisioned an all-encompassing denial of bail to anyone accused of murder. They felt to settle for anything else was to deny Zachary's importance and the relevance of his life. In March 2010, the Bagbys pressed the bill once more before the Commons justice and human rights committee, and it finally became a law in December of 2010. The criminal code was changed to allow courts to refuse bail for any person accused of a serious crime who has a child under the age of 18 years-old.

To the Bagbys, the law means that Parliament admits the previous bail structure had a hand in why Zachary died. It was a win for them in more ways than one. It was a win for Andrew and for Zachary as well and the many people who fought in the battle to make the law real. The bill allowed the Bagbys some peace of mind if nothing else. Their wounds, of course, will never heal completely, but with the knowledge of the bill's passage, at least they could know it wouldn't happen again to some other poor soul.

As much progress as the new law shows, the years since its passage have still been troublesome for Canada's child welfare system. The bill spurred on by Zachary's death was only a drop in the proverbial bucket when considering the magnitude of the crisis still happening in 2015.

Each year has brought some atrocious crime against a child who was under the protection of the country's child welfare programs. Much like Zachary, the brutish 2013 torturing and death of Jeffrey Baldwin led to changes in how the system designates custody of minors to relatives in Canada. The Catholic Children's Aid Society removed young Jeffrey and his older sister from their parents after abuse accusations surfaced. The children were placed in the care of their maternal grandparents, Elva Bottineau and Norman Kidman, already convicted of child abuse, who systematically tortured and abused Jeffrey until he died of malnutrition and septic shock in relation to his injuries. A bronze statue of Jeffrey as Superman was later erected in his honor. After this case's tragic ending became public, stricter family research, criminal record and background checks, and the same rigorous standards non-related foster parents must satisfy are now required of family members.

Early 2014 brought the heart-wrenching case of Phoenix Sinclair [16] to light. The investigation into her death was the largest public inquiry to delve into the child welfare system the city of Manitoba had ever been involved in. Upon her birth, she was immediately removed from her parents', Samantha Kematch's and Steve Sinclair's, guardianship. They had been deemed unable to successfully parent and Samantha had a previous child who was a permanent ward of the state. Phoenix was first placed in a temporary shelter and then with a foster family. Her parents were eventually granted visitation rights and then full custody. It didn't take long, however, before things turned sour between Samantha and Steve, and after several domestic violence calls, the pair split with Steve remaining to care for Phoenix and her sister Echo.

The child services department was called several times while Steve was considered the primary caregiver of the girls. Echo died of a respiratory infection in 2001. Phoenix, according to child services records, spent the majority of her time at a family friend's house, Kim Edwards. In 2003, Phoenix was brought to the hospital for a piece of Styrofoam that had been lodged in her nose for four months. When hospital and medical staff expressed concern over Steve's ability to properly administer antibiotics and facilitate Phoenix's recuperation, she was moved into the custody of Kim Edwards.

Samantha and her new boyfriend Karl "Wes" McKay received custody of Phoenix in 2004. The couple had a child of their own shortly after as well as two children of his from a previous marriage. Time after time, child services opened cases due to reports of neglect just to close them soon after. In 2005, McKay, who often played violent, sadistic games with Phoenix where he choked her unconscious, beat the 5-year-old girl for over 15 minutes until she stopped breathing. McKay's 12-year-old son waited for him to leave the room and checked on Phoenix to discover she had died. The couple threw her body in a landfill and continued life as usual, cashing welfare checks in Phoenix's name until the 12-year-old son told his mother what had happened to Phoenix and she called the police. Commissioner Ted Hughes released the inquiry report in January 2014 where he stated "deeply rooted issues" in the child welfare system were present and cited 62 suggestions imperative to improve the programs.

Seven-year-old Katelynn Sampson's horrific 2008 death shocked Canada. Katelynn's heroin-addicted mother gave her to a friend who became her legal guardian, Donna Irving and her boyfriend, Warren Johnson. The pair was granted full legal guardianship despite repeated and well-known arrests for narcotics, prostitution and extreme violence. The pair beat and tortured the girl to death. She died with more than 70 injuries to her small body.

The couple initially tried to get rid of Katelynn, telling authorities, social workers and the girl's family members that she was a problem, that they didn't like her and couldn't afford her. Nothing was done, however, and eventually the couple used her as a punching bag, increasing the beating when a letter came which they thought meant no more state payments for the girl. Young Katelynn lay dying of her internal injuries and the two went to the beer store and took a leisurely walk. Upon returning and discovering her death, Irving called 911 and reported Katelynn had choked on a piece of bread. When police searched her room, they found a scrap of paper with the words *I am an awful girl that's why no one wants me* printed on it 62 times. Katelynn had missed enormous amounts of school, and when she did go, it was always with bruises. Teachers and the principal reported the abuse but nothing was ever done.

Add these deaths to the exorbitant amount who die quietly in daycare each year and the realization dawns that children's safety issues are far undervalued in Canada.

In 2014, Carol Chafe, [17] Newfoundland and Labrador's advocate for children and youth, told a CTV news reporter that she had been unaware of 35 deaths of children under government care. It came to her attention only after another reporter had filed a request for information from the administration. She was in mid-investigation on six other deaths she'd gained knowledge of through media. While the deaths were not suspicious, the fact that higher-ups were not notified is cause for concern.

Young, innocent Zachary's death, did not solve the problem of Canada's child care system, but it undoubtedly made way for badly needed change and opened the door for more grassroots lobbying for important child care bills.

The documentary is the main testament to the tragic story of Andrew and Zachary. The amazing film originally meant to console Zachary did so much more than ever expected. The film's detailed account helped to get the bill the support it needed to pass into a law but also provided great support for the mourning parents of Andrew Bagby and grandparents of Zachary. The film is complete with heartwarming testimony from Andrew's friends and family of what an amazing, kind and lovable person that Andrew was in life. The film allowed a glimpse into Andrew's life and how he influenced others. After the whole ordeal was over, Kathleen and David were left feeling utterly alone, so the friends and fellow family of Andrew all commended the Bagby parents on their bravery in the face of an incident that would devastate most people and their dedication to making change against an overwhelmingly damaged child protection system. The film's success has brought the information about the incident all over the U.S. and Canada, ensuring that his memory will live on in the hearts of everyone who witnesses the touching film.

Kate and David Bagby eventually moved back to the United States, but they continue to fight for the rights of children and the restructuring of bail laws [18] in Canada. By continuing the struggle long after their personal hell has ended, they fight to keep Zachary and Andrew's cause and therefore their memory alive and well and help to prevent similar occurrences.

Shirley Turner's older children are now adults living in the Newfoundland area. They have gone on to live quiet lives in the shadow of their mother and brother's horrific deaths.

The memory of Andrew and Zachary and the impact they had on not only the lives of those who knew them, but also those who need them most will live forever. The pain that the Bagbys felt did not destroy them but instead spurred a change in the world. Those who knew him feel Andrew would be very proud of that.

Acknowledgements

I want to thank my editor and proof-readers. I can't thank you enough for your ongoing support:

- Kelly

Bettye McKee

Lorrie Suzanne Phillippe

Amanda Hutchins

Marlene Fabregas

Darlene Horn

Ron Steed

June Julie Dechman

Karen Emberton Spear

Katherine McCarthy

Charlotte Fawkes Ellis

Robyn MacEachern

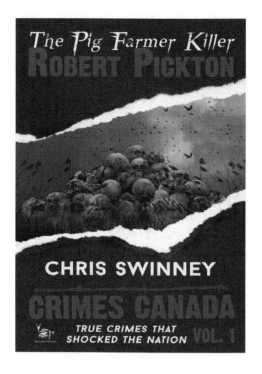

by **Chris Swinney**

Robert Pickton inherited a pig farm worth a million dollars and used his wealth to lure skid row hookers to his farm where he confessed to murdering 49 female victims, dismembering them and feeding their body parts to his pigs which he supplied to Vancouver area restaurants.

WITH PHOTOS

Marc Lepine: The Montreal Massacre

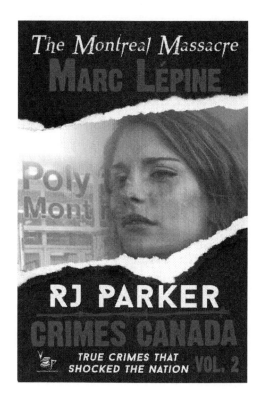

by **RJ Parker**

With extreme hatred in his heart against feminism, an act that feminists would label 'gynocide', a heavily armed Marc Lépine entered the University École Polytechnique de Montreal and, after allowing the male students to leave, systematically murdered 14 female students.

But what motivated Lépine to carry out this heinous crime? Mass murderer, madman, cold-blooded killer, misogynist, political zealot? Or was he simply another desperate person frustrated with his powerless status in this world?

WITH PHOTOS

Paul Bernardo and Karla Homolka: The Ken and Barbie Killers

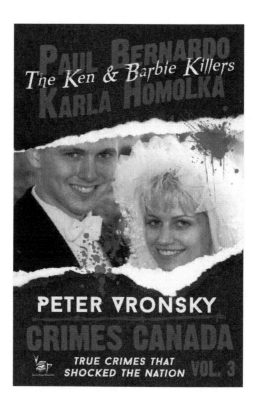

by **Dr. Peter Vronsky**

"**WARNING** - This book contains police and court transcripts of audio and descriptions of extremely graphic sexual violence contained in videotapes made by the perpetrators."

Paul Bernardo and Karla Homolka were so perfectly iconic as a newlywed couple that they were dubbed "Ken and Barbie". But their marriage had a dark side involving sex, death, and videotape. The 'perfect couple' first raped and murdered Karla's little sister and then kidnapped teenage schoolgirls whom they enslaved, raped, tortured and killed while gleefully recording themselves on video doing it. Vronsky will take you on the journey from the Scarborough Rapist (Bernardo) to Bordelais (Homolka's current last name) and her return to Canada in October 2014 from the island of Gaudeloupe where she lived for several years with her husband and three children.

WITH PHOTOS

To view past and future books in the Crimes Canada collection, please click *HERE*

About the Author

Kelly Banaski is a true crime writer and blogger at www.thewomancondemned.comwhere she writes about her attempts at prison reform, and the interactions it allows with many of America's death row and, most infamous women. Her unusual childhood raised by a career criminal and sometimes fugitive, has granted her a unique perspective on inmate issues that manifests itself in many of her inmate relationships. These personal relationships that develop, often result in stories that no other writers have access to.

Kelly entered a writing contest for the second annual *Serial Killers True Crime Anthology, 2015, Volume II*, and was selected over several other entries.

Connect with Kelly:

Blog: www.TheWomanCondemned.com

Website: www.KellyBanaski.com

Twitter: @WriteLikeAMutha

Facebook:
https://www.Facebook.com/WomanCondemned

Table of Contents

Endnotes

1   http://dvd.netflix.com/Movie/Dear-Zachary-A-Letter-to-a-Son-About-His-Father/70095159

2   http://www.childandyouthadvocate.nf.ca/pdfs/turner-v1.pdf

3   http://www.decision-making-confidence.com/female-sociopaths.html

4   http://www.amazon.com/Just-Like-Father-Liane-Leedom/dp/0977801306

5   http://www.amazon.com/Women-Who-Kill-RJ-Parker-ebook/dp/B0061XRYZ4

6   http://www.duhaime.org/LegalDictionary/M/MoralInsanity.aspx

7   http://www.oregoncounseling.org/Handouts/PsychopathicPersonality.htm

8   http://www.amazon.com/Dance-Devil-Memoir-Murder-Loss/dp/1552638197

9   http://www.cyclopaedia.info/wiki/Andrew-Bagby

10 http://www.childandyouthadvocate.nf.ca/pdfs/turner-v2.pdf

11 http://en.wikipedia.org/wiki/Murder_of_Zachary_Turner

12 http://www.utpjournals.press/doi/abs/10.3138/cpp.38.1.55?journalCode=cpp

13 http://www.thetelegram.com/News/Local/2013-08-17/article-3354080/Scarred-by-murder/1

14 http://www.cbc.ca/news/canada/newfoundland-labrador/no-need-for-zachary-turner-to-die-death-review-1.596561

15 http://www.canadiancrc.com/Zachary_Turner.aspx

16 http://en.wikipedia.org/wiki/Phoenix_Sinclair

17 http://www.ctvnews.ca/canada/n-l-s-child-advocate-not-aware-of-most-deaths-since-2009-1.2022498

18 http://news.nationalpost.com/2013/08/09/after-canadian-mother-killed-herself-and-their-only-grandchild-u-s-couple-started-10-year-fight-to-change-canadas-bail-laws/

14904617R00056

Printed in Great Britain
by Amazon.co.uk, Ltd.,
Marston Gate.